Henny Youngman's
888 GREATEST INSULTS

Henny Youngman's
888 GREATEST INSULTS

Illustrated by
Debra Solomon

WINGS BOOKS
New York • Avenel, New Jersey

This 1995 edition is published by Wings Books,
distributed by Random House Value Publishing, Inc.,
40 Engelhard Avenue, Avenel, New Jersey 07001,
by arrangement with the author.

Random House
New York • Toronto • London • Sydney • Auckland

Printed and bound in the United States of America

Library of Congress Cataloging-in-Publication Data

Youngman, Henny.
Henny Youngman's 888 greatest insults / by Henny Youngman;
illustrated by Debra Solomon.
p.   cm.
ISBN 0-517-10189-0
1. Invective—Humor. I. Title. II. Title: Henny Youngman's
eight hundred and eighty eight greatest insults.
PN6231.I65Y68   1995
818'.5402—dc20   94-31902
                                                          CIP

8   7   6   5   4   3   2   1

CONTENTS

He looks like he got dressed in front of an airplane propeller.

Appearances Are Deceiving

There's only one thing wrong with you. You're visible.

Was that suit made to order? Where were you at the time?

You look like a talent scout for a cemetery.

When you get up in the morning, who puts you together?

For short people: I've been looking low and low for you.

I can't forget the first time I laid eyes on you—and don't think
I haven't tried.

I never forget a face, and in your case I'll remember both of them.

Who shines your suits?

Beauty always comes from within—within jars, tubes, and compacts.

She wanted a gift to go with her looks—so I bought her a set of
horse shoes.

Henny Youngman's 888 Greatest Insults

Sit down; you make the place look shabby!

If I were you, I'd return that face to Abbey rents.

There's a pair of shoes with three heels.

There's one good thing about being bald—it's neat.

He dresses like an unmade bed!

He was the only man ever kicked out of the army for looking like a one-man slum.

Next time you give your clothes away—stay in them.

Why don't you start neglecting your appearance? Then maybe it'll go away.

There's a guy who lives alone and looks it.

Appearances Are Deceiving

Some women have natural beauty along with a special talent for making the worst of it.

In the beauty parlor my wife patronizes, the talk alone is enough to curl one's hair.

A beautician is a person who puts a price on a women's head.

A beauty parlor is a place where men are rare and women well-done.

Is that a suit you have on, or are you dancing with someone?

Broadcloth is the cloth used to make girls' dresses.

Who gave you that tie? Someone angry at you?

Fashion is a racket for selling clothes.

The hardest thing on a woman's clothes is another woman.

That's a nice dress. You must wear it sometime.

Sign in a dress shop: Buy now—our skirts are going up.

Statistics are like a bikini bathing suit. What they reveal is suggestive, but what they conceal is vital.

She has no more on her body than on her mind.

I got my wife a housecoat to wear around the house—it fits either of them.

My wife dresses like she's fleeing from a burning building.

My wife's new evening dress is more gone than gown.

After seeing her in slacks I stopped calling my wife "the little woman."

My wife will spend $25 on a slip and then be annoyed if it shows.

Give some women an inch and they'll wear it for a dress.

The call them "unmentionables" because they're nothing to speak of.

My daughter wears too much of not enough.

My daughter looks as if her clothes were thrown on her with a pitchfork.

In an amber dress with a white collar she looked like
a short beer with legs.

Women over sixty aren't just dressed—they're upholstered.

Today's teenager goes to the beach to try to outstrip the other girls.

My wife dressed like a lady—Lady Godiva.

Her suit looks like a million dollars—all green and wrinkled.

When my wife wears a red dress she looks like a bow-legged fire engine.

Her dress looked pretty good considering the shape it was on.

Actually I'm wearing this suit to pay off an election bet.

I found out what my wife wanted with six dresses—six pairs of shoes.

I'd like to see my wife wear her dresses a little longer—about a year longer.

My girlfriend is a window dresser—never pulls her shades down.

If a man can't see why you wear a strapless gown, you shouldn't.

She shows a lot of style, and her style shows a lot of woman.

Appearances Are Deceiving

My wife dresses to kill and cooks the same way.

I told my wife her nylons were wrinkled—but she wasn't wearing any.

The only thing holding up her dress is a city ordinance.

With that dress I can't tell if she's trying to catch a cold or a man.

She wears tight clothing to squeeze out the last ounce of value.

When a man's socks and tie match, he's wearing a present.

My wife doesn't know which dress she doesn't want until she buys it.

He got a very expensive suit for a ridiculous figure. His!

There was something dove-like about her—she was pigeon-toed.

She had a heart of gold—and teeth to match.

He can swat flies with his ears.

She thinks she's a siren, but she looks more like a false alarm.

He shaves with cold water, because hot water steams up his mirror.

The only time my son washes his ears is when he eats watermelon.

The way she keeps her eyebrows takes a lot of pluck.

Her eyes are so bad, she has to wear contact lenses to see her glasses.

My eyes were never good and I have a wife to prove it.

He's not working up a steam; he's generating a fog.

I won't say she was ugly—but it was love at first fright.

Appearances Are Deceiving

My girlfriend is so ritzy, she has alligator bags under her eyes.

She's got patriotic eyes—blue, with red whites.

My wife has dyed by her own hand.

She's a cross between a brunette and a drugstore.

To a bald man dandruff is a thrill.

Everyone has hair problems: with women it's tent, with men 'tain't.

I just discovered a new birth control device. My wife takes off her makeup.

My wife looks her best in the same old thing—the dark.

A snob is a person who was born with his face lifted.

She should go to a plastic surgeon to have her nose lowered.

There's a lot less to some people than meets the eye.

Eat, Drink & Be Bleary

Four drunks looked at him, they took the pledge.

If they can make penicillin out of moldy bread, surely they can make something out of you.

He's a real good egg, and you know where eggs come from.

I'm going to name my first ulcer after you.

You're the kind of person I would like to have over when I have the measles.

He has more crust than a pie factory.

He doesn't get ulcers, he gives them.

Lot's of people owe a lot to him—ulcers, nausea, diarrhea.

My doctor always looks like a cheerleader for the morgue.

If you were alive, you'd be a very sick man.

The last time he was in a hospital, he got get-well cards from all the nurses.

An appendix is what you have taken out before the doctor decides it is your gall bladder.

I know a fellow with a real drinking problem—his wife insists on accompanying him to the bar.

Talk about depression—my neighbor shaves before weighing himself on the bathroom scale.

By going without lunch and dinner, almost anyone can afford breakfast.

My wife won't eat anything that starts with the letter "Z".

My wife is always on a diet—but she's just a wishful shrinker.

My wife takes her reducing pills in a chocolate malted.

My wife keeps young by dieting, jogging, and lying about her age.

Eat, Drink & Be Bleary

To lose weight my wife went to a diet doctor. In one week she lost $100.

I've got an easy diet. I never eat when my wife is talking.

I don't drink to my wife—I drink because of her.

He breathed on the back of her neck and bleached her hair.

Not only do I like to drink Zombies—I married one.

If a mosquito bit him, it would die of alcohol-poisoning.

An alcoholic is someone you don't like who drinks as much as you do.

I'm not saying he drinks, but everybody calls him a "ham on rye."

Two drunks looked at my wife and took the pledge.

Alcohol is like success: both are all right until they go to your head.

His idea of frozen food is Scotch on the rocks.

We make breakfast together. She makes toast, and I scrape it.

Dad is a joiner by trade. If anyone orders a drink, he joins them.

My wife is such a bad cook, she blushes after every meal.

My wife will go anywhere for dinner, except to the kitchen.

My wife enjoys cooking—especially when it's done in a restaurant.

When my wife makes Jello, I get a lump in my throat.

One thing about my wife's coffee—it's not habit-forming.

What my wife doesn't know about cooking would fill a book
—a cookbook.

No woman is as old as she looks before breakfast.

I drink several cups of water a day—my wife calls it coffee.

Eat, Drink & Be Bleary

My wife's coffee is so weak it can't even hold the sugar.

When my wife's away I do wonderful things with leftovers—I throw them out.

My wife needs a full day to make a cup of instant coffee.

I once broke a tooth on my wife's gravy.

The menu is the list of dishes the restaurant has just run out of.

A chef's idea of decor is parsley.

Only one thing is bigger than my wife's appetite: her stomach.

I don't mind my wife serving TV dinners, but now she's serving re-runs.

In a restaurant, my favorite dish is a clean one.

I think my wife has been getting her recipes out of *Popular Mechanics*.

Her cooking is so bad, our garbage can got ulcers.

She fed a stray dog, and it never left—it couldn't move.

Some people can't boil water. My wife can. She calls it soup.

My wife has a great way to keep food costs down—her cooking.

When my wife makes coffee it's grounds for divorce.

My wife's food can cure you of anything, including life.

Her grub tastes like one.

Her food is for thought—it's certainly not for eating.

On our honeymoon my wife burned the toast—so I wouldn't notice the coffee.

My wife's life is a bed of neuroses.

Money can't buy health, but it can buy a car for the doctor's wife.

Eat, Drink & Be Bleary

My wife has had every ailment and disease shown on television.

My wife has a talent for organ recitals—about her operations.

A hypochondriac is always sure to have some ailment in mind.

My wife is always on pills and needles.

One tourniquet that stops circulation is a wedding ring.

One illness you can catch from a hypochondriac is a pain in the neck.

If an actor sneezes on television my wife think's she's caught a cold.

Many women who are the picture of health are just painted that way.

My wife's usual greeting is "Good moaning."

A frustrated hypochondriac is one who is allergic to medicine.

Wives suffer as many ulcers as husbands do. The same ones.

One new miracle drug is so strong you have to be in perfect health to use it.

People who have insomnia lie awake all night for an hour.

The best thing for halitosis is lockjaw.

Tell my wife how healthy she looks and you've made a mortal enemy.

Some people can see viruses in the milk of human kindness.

My wife's not a cook—she's an arsonist.

The idea for whiskey sours came from a look at my wife's face.

Give a woman an inch—and immediately the entire family is on a diet.

Not only has my wife kept her girlish figure—she doubled it.

Eat, Drink & Be Bleary

Either my wife goes on a diet or we'll have to let out the couch.

I've got a wife that dresses to kill, and cooks that way, too.

My wife can't cook. Last night she burned the potato salad.

If the bravest are the tenderest, this steak came from a coward.

My wife always gives you a preamble to her constitution.

My wife's health has me worried. It's always good.

My wife went on a diet, but all she lost was her sense of humor.

No Place Like Home . . . Relatively Speaking

There's no place like home, and I, for one, am glad of it.

He was born at home but when his mother saw him she went
to the hospital.

He's hoping for a lucky stroke—his rich uncle's.

Is your family happy? Or do you go home at night?

I wish somebody would kidnap you—but who would they contact?

A bachelor is a guy who thinks planned parenthood is living with
his mother.

Having a big family around is a good way to make sure there will always
be someone to answer the phone—and forget the message.

She got her good looks from her mother, who owns a beauty parlor.

When our home burned down, it was
the first time the food was hot.

Henny Youngman's 888 Greatest Insults

My brother-in-law's mind is a regular scheme engine.

The only time my brother is on the level is when he's sleeping.

I've got two wonderful children—and two out of five isn't too bad.

Some kids would rather steal hub caps than third base.

A boy is a noise with some dirt on it.

A child is a thing that stands halfway between an adult and a TV set.

My neighborhood was so tough, Santa came up from the sewer.

I've had gray hair since I was born. Mother powdered the wrong place.

Children should be seen and not had.

He must get his brains from his mother. I still have mine.

Every Christmas she hung up her stockings, but all she ever got
was a run.

Misery is when Christmas has come and gone, but your relatives haven't.

No Place Like Home . . . Relatively Speaking

Christmas is a holiday that always comes a month before arriving.

Christmas bills are the real morning after.

We had a power failure in our house. My wife lost her voice.

Give a man a couple of loud ties and it's Christmas.

By the time I found a place to park, Christmas was over.

The only time my wife stops talking is when her mother starts.

My wife has a very sad parrot. He's never had a chance to talk.

My brother-in-law has a new position—he's standing up.

My mother-in-law is as stuck-up as a billboard.

My brother-in-law is as refined as a cabbage.

My brother-in-law is a contact man—all con and no tact.

My family acquired polish by drinking it.

Some men are born lucky; others have large families.

Talk about a failure! My uncle robbed a bank just to feel wanted.

My mother-in-law has a nice open face—open day and night.

I miss my wife's cooking—every chance I get.

My uncle is a cannibal—he's been living on us for twenty years.

My brother is so high strung he joined a circus.

My marriage is a give and take proposition. I give and she takes.

I admit that I married my wife for her money—and boy, do I earn it.

Relatives are people who are satisfied to live within your means.

A relative is a spending unit.

I got this dog for my wife. I'd like to make a trade like that every day.

A genius is a stupid kid with very happy grandparents.

A Sunday picnic with the kids is no picnic.

These days it's difficult for a girl to look as young as her mother.

She's the picture of her father, and the sound track of her mother.

My brother-in-law has an allergy. He's allergic to work.

Home is a place to stay while the car is being serviced.

There's no place like home if you haven't got the money to go out.

My home is my castle—while my wife is out shopping.

First a man buys a home—then he buys a car to get away from it.

There's no place like home—thank heaven.

There's no place like home, which is why I go out nights.

There's no place like home, particularly when you're looking for trouble.

No Place Like Home . . . Relatively Speaking

My hotel is popular as a resort. A last resort.

In my hotel everything is cold but the ice water.

My room has natural air-conditioning—a broken window.

My room is so small the mice are hunchbacked.

My room is so small every time I bend over I rearrange the furniture.

My room is so small I have to go outside to change my mind.

My room is so small when a dog visited me, it had to wag its tail up and down.

My room is so small I have wall-to-wall furniture.

I get all the hot water I want by asking for soup in the dining room.

Henny Youngman's 888 Greatest Insults

My wife knows my jokes backwards—and tells them that way.

An infant prodigy is a young child whose parents are highly imaginative.

My brother-in-law's life work is to avoid it.

Many people are too lazy to work, but my brother-in-law is too lazy to fish.

The only thing my brother-in-law ever does fast is get tired.

It takes my wife five minutes to boil a three-minute egg.

My brother only opens his mouth to put something in it.

My brother is a miracle worker—it's a miracle he works.

My brother-in-law is as active as a leftover fly in January.

My brother is the family idol. He's been idle for the past five years.

Many a favorite son shows you how blind maternal love is.

I can tell when my wife is lying—if her lips are moving, she is.

No Place Like Home . . . Relatively Speaking

My room is so small when the sun came in, I had to get out.

My room is so small when I closed the door, the doorknob pinched
my stomach.

My mother-in-law never wipes her opinion off her face.

My brother-in-law thinks the world is against him—and it is.

Arguing with my wife is like trying to read a newspaper in a high wind.

My mother-in-law looks through rose-colored glasses with
a jaundiced eye.

I think my mother-in-law was weaned on a pickle.

There's no place like home, once in a while.

Courtship, Marriage & Other Annoyances

At least he gives his wife something to live for—a divorce.

You know, I'd like to send you a Valentine, but I haven't figured out how to wrap lace around a time bomb.

Look at him, sex takes a holiday.

The difference in the aging process in men and women is that men get sadder and wiser but women get sadder and wider.

Age makes wine worth more and women less.

Middle age is the time in life when a woman's curves turn into circles.

The only way a middle-aged woman can hold her school-girl figure is in fond memory.

Girls are so knowing these days that birds and bees study them.

The only thing that makes my wife late is an appointment.

When I win an argument with my wife, the argument is not over.

I know a real loser. The day he got married he carried his bride over the threshold and got a hernia.

Sixty percent of the men cheat in America. The rest cheat in Europe.

Generally speaking, my wife is generally speaking.

My wife is breathtaking—every few hours she stops talking to take a breath.

My wife can talk fifty percent faster than anyone can listen.

I've never seen my wife's tongue. It moves too fast.

My wife even talks to herself—to be sure of getting in the last word.

My wife never has the last word—she never gets to it.

My wife has a chronic speech impediment—palpitation of the tongue.

Courtship, Marriage & Other Annoyances

Each morning my wife brushes her teeth and sharpens her tongue.

The only time my wife suffers in silence is when the phone is
out of order.

My wife makes up her face more easily than her mind.

A girl knows when the right man comes along—he notices her.

How can I live without her? Cheaper.

To fall in love you must have an open mind—a hole in the head.

Real courage is marrying a three-times-widowed woman.

For years I suffered from a pain in the neck, so I'm finally divorcing her.

Our divorce was the result of unpleasant relations—such as her parents.

Henny Youngman's 888 Greatest Insults

I believed in dreams until I married my wife.

She didn't marry me for my money—she divorced me for it.

Some husbands are very versatile—they can't do anything.

There is no man so bad that a woman cannot make him worse.

When a man needs a friend he often makes a mistake and gets a wife.

She's a home-loving girl, but she does some loving in the car, too.

Getting a girl is easy—losing her is the real job.

My girl is so bashful, she goes into the closet to change her mind.

Her kiss speaks volumes—but it's far from a first edition.

Courtship, Marriage & Other Annoyances

Almost any girl can talk rings around a jewelry store.

My girl can't swim a stroke, but she knows every dive in town.

"Girls" are what women over 45 call each other.

The story of her popularity can be summed up in one word: "Yes."

Girls with hidden charms do their best not to hide them.

What a hairdo! It's like a floor mop in a high wind.

My girl's the type to take home to Mother—when Mother isn't home.

My girlfriend looks like a million—every year of it.

The only sign of toil on her hand is her engagement ring.

She turned my head with her charm, and my stomach with her cooking.

The only time some girls say "Stop" is in a telegram.

My girl isn't complex—anyone can grasp her.

My girl looks good in everything—but a mirror.

My girl is a vision in the evening and a sight in the morning.

Girlhood is sixty pounds ago.

For twenty years my wife and I were happy—then we met.

Kissing shortens life—single life, that is.

My nephew is so boring girls kiss him to shut his mouth.

I got a warmer kiss from the high school principal when I graduated.

Kissing is still practiced in England—but is it worth the trip?

I take my wife everywhere I go—I hate to kiss her good-bye.

I'll never forget my first wife's kisses—like opening a refrigerator.

Marriage is just another union that defies management.

Love makes the world go 'round—looking for a job.

Courtship, Marriage & Other Annoyances

Love is a disease usually cured by marriage.

Love at first sight never happens before breakfast.

A man in love shows great ingenuity in making a fool of himself.

Puppy love is the prelude to a dog's life.

Some men fall in love, but they get out of it by marrying the girl.

I knew it was puppy love because her nose was always cold and damp.

It was love at first sight. She first saw him in his Mercedes.

Everyone has someone, but all I have is you.

Love is a feeling that makes a woman make a man make a fool of himself.

The love that passeth all understanding is on television.

Man worships woman, and then sacrifices himself at the altar.

It's love when she looks at him as if he's a coat she can't afford.

She fell in love with me. She wrote every week—for one week.

When a man is engaged, the lucky woman is the girl's mother.

Beginners' luck is happiness during the first two weeks after marriage.

The thing my wife finds hardest to do is give in.

I'm leaving my wife because of another woman—her mother.

My wife isn't talking to me—and I'm in no mood to interrupt her.

The only thing my wife doesn't know is why she married me.

My wife is like an angel, always harping on something.

Love is the wine of life, and marriage is the morning after.

Love flatters your ego while it flattens your wallet.

Courtship, Marriage & Other Annoyances

I take her everywhere, but it's no use. She always finds her way back.

Courtship is love's sweet dream—it's followed by marriage,
the alarm clock.

Opposites attract. Poor girls are always looking for a rich husband.

She leads a conventional life—she shows up at all the conventions.

An onion, or a husband, can make any woman weep.

A wife is a former sweetheart.

I have the best wife in the country. Sometimes I wish
she'd stay there.

I have a way with my wife, but it's seldom my own.

Love makes time pass, and time makes love pass.

I'm Not Saying He's Stingy, But . . .

I'm not saying he's stingy, but as a freeloader, he's known from host to host.

I'm not saying he's stingy, but he does have a burglar alarm on his garbage can.

I'm not saying he's stingy, but he makes every dollar go as far as possible —and every girl, too.

I'm not saying he's stingy, but he won't even spend the time of day.

I'm not saying he's stingy, but of all the near-relatives in the family, he's the closest.

I'm not saying he's stingy, but if he ever found a box of corn plasters, he'd start wearing tight shoes.

I'm not saying he's stingy, but he even washes his paper plates.

I'm not saying he's stingy, but he learned to read Braille so he can read in the dark.

I'm not saying he's stingy, but he wouldn't even spend Christmas.

I'm not saying he's stingy, but after shaking your hand
he counts his fingers.

I'm not saying he's stingy, but he puts boric acid on his grapefruit to get a free eyewash.

I'm not saying he's stingy, but the reason he's so clean is that he's been sponging for years.

I'm not saying he's stingy, but he does his Christmas shopping surly.

I'm not saying he's stingy, but he thinks the world owes him a giving.

I'm not saying he's stingy, but he never takes anything but a sponge bath.

I'm not saying he's stingy, but he tosses quarter tips around like manhole covers.

I'm not saying he's stingy, but at the Last Supper he would have asked for separate checks.

I'm not saying he's stingy, but he is saving all his toys for his second childhood.

I'm not saying he's stingy, but his money talks with a stutter.

I'm Not Saying He's Stingy, But . . .

I'm not saying he's stingy, but he has a physical handicap—he's hard-of-spending.

I'm not saying he's stingy, but before counting his money he gets drunk so he'll see double.

I'm not saying he's stingy, but even if he was in a canoe he wouldn't tip.

I'm not saying he's stingy, but for an ice pack he only uses one cube.

I'm not saying he's stingy, but he keeps a moth as a pet because it only eats holes.

I'm not saying he's stingy, but he keeps his piggy bank in a safe deposit box.

I'm not saying he's stingy, but he always takes long steps to save on shoe leather.

I'm not saying he's stingy, but he married a skinny girl so he could get a small wedding ring.

I'm not saying he's stingy, but he always wears mittens so money won't slip through his fingers.

I'm not saying he's stingy, but he bought his daughter a doll house with a mortgage on it.

I'm not saying he's stingy, but he called up his girl friend to find out which night she was free.

I'm not saying he's stingy, but he's waiting for the Encyclopedia Britannica to come out in paperback.

I'm not saying he's stingy, but he only goes to drive-in movies in the daytime.

I'm Not Saying He's Stingy, But . . .

I'm not saying he's stingy, but he never enjoys dessert in a restaurant; it's too close to the check.

I'm not saying he's stingy, but he only rides the bus during rush hours to get his clothes pressed.

I'm not saying he's stingy, but he rethreads his old shoelaces.

I'm not saying he's stingy, but he decided to become a divorce lawyer— so he can get a free woman.

I'm not saying he's stingy, but he quit playing golf when he lost his ball.

I'm not saying he's stingy, but he's tighter than the top olive in the bottle.

I'm not saying he's stingy, but it's a sure sign of summer when he throws away his Christmas tree.

I'm not saying he's stingy, but he got his money the hoard way.

I'm not saying he's stingy, but he's satisfied to let the rest of the world go buy.

I'm not saying he's stingy, but in a nightclub, he always sits with his back to the check.

I'm not saying he's stingy, but he'd skin a flea for its hide and tallow.

I'm not saying he's stingy, but he drinks with impunity—in fact, with anyone who'll buy.

I'm not saying he's stingy, but he's so tight, when he winks, his kneecaps move.

I'm not saying he's stingy, but he takes corners on two wheels to save his tires.

I'm not saying he's stingy, but when he goes on a week's vacation, all he spends is seven days.

I'm not saying he's stingy, but he's first to put his hand in his pocket— and keep it there.

I'm not saying he's stingy, but he's one guy who knows how to hold his liquor.

I'm not saying he's stingy, but he always counts his money
in front of a mirror so he won't cheat.

I'm not saying he's stingy, but he's always living within his relatives' means.

I'm not saying he's stingy, but he throws money around like a man without arms.

I'm not saying he's stingy, but the only thing he ever gave away was a secret.

I'm not saying he's stingy, but anyone can borrow his lawn mower—it has a coin slot on it.

I'm not saying he's stingy, but he wouldn't even buy happiness if he had to pay a luxury tax on it.

I'm not saying he's stingy, but after a blood test he demanded his blood sample back.

I'm Not Saying He's Stingy, But . . .

I'm not saying he's stingy, but when he pays you a compliment, he asks for a receipt.

I'm not saying he's stingy, but he orders asparagus and leaves the waiter the tips.

I'm not saying he's stingy, but when everyone else gives three cheers he gives two.

I'm not saying he's stingy, but he won't even let you borrow trouble.

I'm not saying he's stingy, but he had a brass band at his wedding—he put it on his bride's finger.

I'm not saying he's stingy, but to save money on his honeymoon—he went on it alone.

I'm not saying he's stingy, but his motto is: "Money doesn't grow on sprees."

I'm not saying he's stingy, but he'd give you the sleeve out of his vest.

I'm not saying he's stingy, but he has a greater love for specie than the species.

I'm not saying he's stingy, but money flows from him like drops of blood.

I'm not saying he's stingy, but he used the same calendar, year after year.

I'm not saying he's stingy, but he believes that charity begins at home—and should stay there.

I'm not saying he's stingy, but he won't even tip his hat.

I'm not saying he's stingy, but he takes his kids' glasses off when they're not looking at anything.

I'm not saying he's stingy, but he's the kind of guy who takes things for gratis.

I'm not saying he's stingy, but you can always find him with his best friend—his bankroll.

I'm not saying he's stingy, but he has all of his clothes tailored with one-way pockets.

I'm not saying he's stingy, but he weighs 185 pounds—155 pounds without his money belt.

I'm Not Saying He's Stingy, But . . .

I'm not saying he's stingy, but he got married in his own backyard so his chickens could get the rice.

I'm not saying he's stingy, but he dry cleans Kleenex.

I'm not saying he's stingy, but he remarried his wife so he wouldn't have to pay any more alimony.

I'm not saying he's stingy, but the only time he puts his hands in his pockets is on very cold days.

I'm not saying he's stingy, but the only thing he ever spends on a girl is passion.

I'm not saying he's stingy, but last night he took his date out to see a fire.

I'm not saying he's stingy, but he takes his electric razor to the office to recharge it.

I'm not saying he's stingy, but he would never even pass the buck.

I'm not saying he's stingy, but the only thing he ever paid was a compliment.

I'm not saying he's stingy, but the only thing he ever took out was his teeth.

I'm not saying he's stingy, but he thinks he's treating when he pays his own check.

I'm not saying he's stingy, but he took his kids out of school because they had to pay attention.

I'm not saying he's stingy, but he won't even give his wife an argument.

I'm not saying he's stingy, but when he feels sick he goes to the stationery store and reads get-well cards.

I'm not saying he's stingy, but he not only pinches pennies, he pets them.

I'm not saying he's stingy, but the only work he's ever done is freeload.

I'm Not Saying He's Stingy, But . . .

I'm not saying he's stingy, but his pockets always outlast the rest
of his suit.

I'm not saying he's stingy, but he once gave a penny to a blind man—he
needed a pencil.

I'm not saying he's stingy, but he fed his cat salted peanuts so it would
drink water instead of milk.

I'm not saying he's stingy, but he is always forgetting, but never
for giving.

I'm not saying he's stingy, but he takes for granted that taking's
for granted.

I'm not saying he's stingy, but he left everything he had to an orphanage
—four children.

I'm not saying he's stingy, but he's so tight that you can hear him squeak
as he goes by.

Money Matters

Taxes may be staggering, but they never go down.

He spends money like water, drip, drip, drip.

What do you give a guy who has nothing?

America is still the land of opportunity. Where else could you earn enough to owe so much?

America is one place where the people have complete control over how they pay their taxes—cash, check, or money order.

Money is something that brushes by you on its way to Washington.

A fool and his money are soon parted—just like the rest of us.

No man is a hero to a bill collector.

Two can live as cheaply as one, but only half as long.

Man cannot live on bread alone—he has to have credit cards.

By the time a man has money to burn, the fire has gone out.

When my wife writes a check, she draws on her imagination.

Money doesn't go very far these days, or come very near.

Money is the route to all evil.

Money talks most when a man marries it.

Money talks, but it doesn't always talk sense.

A borrower is a person who exchanges hot air for cold cash.

Money is what things run into, and people out of.

A happy wife is one who has everything that credit can buy.

The only thing you can do on a shoestring today is trip.

The love of someone else's money is the root of all evil.

Money is all right, but you have to waste a lot of time making it.

Today I'm celebrating an anniversary—I've been broke for seven years.

There are bigger things in life than money—for instance, bills.

Money Matters

Pay as you go, unless you are going for good.

A bargain is anything that only costs twice as much as it did
five years ago.

The man who can't pay as he goes is going too fast.

A man who can afford to pay the interest today doesn't need the loan.

The only kinds of books I really like are checkbooks.

My credit rating is so bad, my cash isn't even accepted.

Our floating currency is a sign of a sinking economy.

Ever notice that by the time you get a raise it's not enough?

If it's a small world, why does it cost so much to run it?

Yesterday I tried to get change for a quarter and it cost me fifty cents.

A dollar goes very fast these days, but not very far.

Two can live as cheaply as one—large family used to.

At today's prices very few people can afford to be poor.

Money isn't everything—but look at how many things it is.

It's easy to save pennies today—what else can you do with them?

Saving money isn't a challenge—it's an out-and-out victory.

Money isn't everything; sometimes it isn't even 99%.

The other fellow's wallet always looks greener.

I give my wife everything credit can buy.

They say you can't take it with you. I can't even afford to go.

Money Matters

Money isn't everything—for one thing, it isn't plentiful.

Money can't buy everything—poverty, for example.

Money isn't everything—usually, it isn't even enough.

My girlfriend's favorite book is Dunn and Bradstreet.

There is nothing as long as a short-term debt.

When a man says money can do anything—he hasn't any.

After paying my taxes, all I have left is a deficit.

What this country needs is a good five-cent quarter.

Money talks, but poverty just pinches.

A dollar saved is a dollar earned, but seldom vice versa.

Today you can't live on love—without refinancing.

Her husband is rich and old—what a combination!

Money only brings misery—but with it you can afford misery.

A financier is always ready to back his decisions with your last cent.

A budget is an attempt to live below your yearnings.

I had a sinking fund—it just went down for the third time.

These days a man can't afford to make a living.

Money is like a sixth sense—you can't use the other five without it.

Money makes a dirty old man a man-about-town.

I've been broke so long that I can't get used to money.

I'm as sound as a dollar—been to a grocery with a dollar lately?

I've got what no millionaire has got—I've got no money.

Money Matters

My wife loves to spend money, but she hasn't any other extravagances.

Money is like men. The tighter it gets, the louder it talks.

To clean up a man must use soft soap.

Sound money is that which talks the loudest.

Some girls marry for money to make their dreams come true.

Some people make money—others earn it.

My uncle is so rich—he begs with two hats.

Anyone who has $100,000 can always find a bargain.

A debutante is a tomato with plenty of lettuce.

Only Americans have mastered the art of being prosperous though broke.

Have you noticed how people who prize an antique for its beauty suddenly find it unsightly when it turns out to be a fake?

The trouble with most antique shops is that their prices are so modern.

If money doesn't grow on trees, how come banks continue to sprout branches?

Today a bargain is anything that is only moderately overpriced.

A bargain is anything you can buy today at yesterday's prices.

Some housewives carefully go over their budgets each month—others just go over them.

Conservatives are people whose minds become unbalanced just because the budget is.

Give some men a free hand and they'll stick it right in your pocket.

My wife just had plastic surgery—I cut up her credit cards.

Money Matters

A millionaire is a billionaire after he pays his taxes.

A philanthropist gives away what he should be giving back.

Some people think money grows on trees—as they did.

My wife brings more bills into the house than a congressman.

Some men are known by their deeds; others by their mortgages.

Considering our national debt, experience is a dear teacher.

The mint makes money first, it's up to us to make it last.

Occupational Hazards

Show me an amateur, and I'll show you a person who is always willing to give you the benefit of his experience.

You have the Midas touch. Everything you touch turns into a muffler.

He should have been an undertaker—he has no use for anyone living.

Show me an accountant, and I'll show you an acrobat who juggles figures and does a balancing act.

Advertising men can give a favorable image to anything except themselves.

Airline travel is hours of boredom interrupted by moments of stark terror.

If the average congressman found himself on an airplane about to crash he would take time to appoint a landing committee.

I hate those speakers who appeal to the emotions by beating the eardrums.

A baby-sitter is a teenager who gets two dollars an hour to eat five dollars'
worth of your food.

Archeology is the science that proves you can't keep a good man down.

An architect makes an old house look better just by talking about the cost of a new one.

The most economical time to hire a baby-sitter is when the refrigerator is about empty.

We have a baby-sitter who feeds the baby at 10, 12, and 2—and herself at 9, 11, and 1.

My boss intends to take it with him. He just bought a fireproof money belt.

Does the button industry subsidize the laundries?

Baking a smaller loaf enables the bakeries to make a larger roll.

Occupational Hazards

A used car salesman has as much conscience as a fox in a hen house.

Crime is getting so bad in some big cities—even the muggers travel in pairs.

Things are so tough in Chicago, one gangster had to let two cops go.

A burglar is a man seeking an opening in the better stores.

Crime may not pay, but hardly anything else does either.

It's beginning to look as if the underworld has gotten on top.

An arsonist is a person who sets the world on fire—in a small way.

A criminal is one who hasn't enough money to hire expensive lawyers.

A criminal is one who gets caught.

Crime doesn't pay—but policemen don't earn much either.

One thing that never works properly after it is fixed is a jury.

In America, we're willing to try anything once—except the criminals.

Today a murderer is assumed innocent until proven insane.

A clue is what the police boast about when they can't find the criminal.

He'd steal a hot stove and come back for the smoke.

The FBI has the most magnificent collection of clues in existence.

Outlaws may be a menace to society, but in-laws are worse.

Highway patrolmen are cops specially trained to examine drivers' licenses.

Crime doesn't pay—or wouldn't if the government ran it.

In most murder cases there is no clue to the whereabouts of the police.

What the police department doesn't know would fill a jail.

The way of the transgressor is hard—for the police to find out.

Hell hath no fury like the lawyer of a woman scorned.

My doctor put his hand on my wallet and asked me to cough.

A siren is a signal used by the police to warn burglars that they are approaching.

I was so ugly when I was born, the doctor slapped my mother.

My doctor has performed over 400 operations—and never cut himself once.

Never argue with a doctor. He has inside information.

A specialist is a doctor who diagnoses your case by feeling your wallet.

My son is thinking of becoming a doctor. He has the handwriting for it.

He's a specialist—an ear, nose, and threat man.

Doctors are those to whom we entrust our lives—and our fortunes.

My mother-in-law has a lousy doctor. The quack saved her life.

A doctor acts like a humanitarian and charges like a plumber.

A specialist is a doctor whose patients can only be sick during office hours.

When my doctor found out what I had, he relieved me of most of it.

My doctor has magic hands. Each time he touches me $50 disappears.

Occupational Hazards

When she worked for a tea company she asked for a coffee break.

My boss has one of those mighty minds—mighty empty.

I know an actor who is so conceited, he had his x-rays retouched.

I was too busy learning the tricks of the trade to learn the trade.

Show me a dentist, and I'll show you a man who runs a filling station.

A finished speaker seldom is.

Some speakers electrify an audience—others gas it.

He needs no introduction—what he needs is a conclusion.

A lecturer is a person who makes talk money.

A jury is twelve people chosen to decide which side has
the better lawyer.

In court, wrangling between lawyers is nine points of the law.

The prouder a man is of his citizenship, the more he evades jury duty.

My brother is a real lawyer—he even named his daughter Sue.

I don't want a lawyer who knows the law, I want one who knows the judge.

Justice often triumphs in spite of all the publicity issued to support it.

A divorce lawyer is the referee in a fight who winds up with the purse.

The last guess of the Supreme Court becomes the law of the land.

If there were no bad people, there would be no good lawyers.

Some men inherit money, some earn it, and some are lawyers.

A judge is a man who ends a sentence with a sentence.

Occupational Hazards

My mother-in-law dislikes jury duty because it's all listening.

He sleeps as soundly as a night nurse on duty.

He puts in a good day's work—but it takes him a week to do it.

My brother is a genius—he can do almost anything except make a living.

The way he handles the truth, he should work for the weather bureau.

My boss follows the straight and narrow-minded path.

My boss is so narrow-minded, he has to stack his ideas vertically.

I hate the kind of hostess whom you have to thank for her hostility.

Everyone has a good word for the boss—they all whisper it.

My boss is always unpleasant, even when you catch him off-guard.

A man never admits he is a physical wreck, except when suing
for damages.

Some people are like blisters—they don't show up until the work is done.

That's Entertainment

The scenery was beautiful, but the actors got in front of it.

The trouble with opera is that there is too much singing.

I'm planning to invite you to my party—there's always room for one bore.

To be an actor and get paid for it is one way of turning conceit into profit.

Amateur contests give people with no talent a chance to prove it.

He's an agent now. He must know talent. He gave up acting.

I often get stage fright—especially when I see an egg or a tomato.

He's comedy relief—he relieves the picture of all its comedy.

Its impact was like the banging together of two dish cloths.

One actor has been divorced four times—he never could hold
an audience.

Hollywood: Where people from Iowa mistake each other for movie stars.

Some promising singers should promise to stop singing.

He's a mastoid of ceremonies—a pain in the neck.

What's worse than Thursday night on television? Thursday afternoon.

The critic was at the opening night incognito—he was awake.

The circus giant was only seven feet tall—he smoked as a kid.

Even his jokes about old jokes are old.

He was one of the greatest actors ever—to clear his throat.

Television has proved that sight has a definite odor.

She was so dumb they had to rehearse her two weeks for a pause.

He sings for charity—and he needs it.

I had 'em in the aisles—heading for the exits.

He's fast on the ad lib—all he has to do is hear it once.

That's Entertainment

She does a peek-a-boo act. The audience peeks, then boos.

The show was so down to earth the critics buried it.

Athletes are not stupid. You have to be plenty smart to get people to pay to see something as boring as sports.

If you want to see a baseball game in the worst way—take your wife along.

Early to bed and early to rise is a sure sign that you're fed up with television.

There are so many foreign cars in Beverly Hills that it has been two years since anyone has been hit above the knees.

A TV mystery is a detective story where the sponsor gets away with murder.

The show had two strikes against it—the seats faced the stage.

Henny Youngman's 888 Greatest Insults

For the first time in my life I envied my feet. They were asleep.

Of a singer: All her high notes are promissory.

Most of today's movies should be pitied, rather than censored.

A critic is a man who knows the way, but can't drive the car.

This country also needs lighter whines.

The critics arrived after the world was created.

Critics are venomous snakes that delight in hissing.

Las Vegas is a strip of lights surrounded by slot machines.

I get a good deal of pleasure out of my garden—mostly out of it.

I mow the lawn when my neighbor's kid practices the piano.

The way I play golf, the greens flags should be at half-mast.

You chase a golf ball when you are too old to chase anything else.

A golfer is a gardener digging up someone else's lawn.

His friends call it madness, he calls it golf.

I'm so used to cheating that when I made a hole-in-one, I put down zero.

On a public golf course, you hit a ball, and a picnic runs out and grabs it.

A Hollywood producer is an ulcer with authority.

In Hollywood, an actress is anybody who's got a dimple.

The happy ending of some movies is the mere fact that they have ended.

One actor likes his new wife enough to hold her over for a second week.

I remember you—you're a graduate of the Don Rickles Charm School.

Zsa Zsa Gabor has been married so many times she has rice marks on her face.

Hollywood executives used to pinch starlets, now they pinch pennies.

Stories about Hollywood marriages should end with a comma.

That's Entertainment

In Hollywood they shoot too much film and not enough actors.

A Hollywood marriage is a good way to spend a weekend.

It's spring in Hollywood when the smog gets greener.

Hollywood: The place bad plays go when they die.

Hollywood: An asylum run by the inmates.

If a man's wife looks like a new woman in Hollywood—she probably is.

Hollywood is a gold rush of dinner jackets.

Hollywood is a sunny spot for shady people.

A silver wedding anniversary in Hollywood means the
twenty-fifth wedding.

The movie industry finds out what you don't like, then gives it to you.

Hollywood is a state of mind surrounded by Los Angeles.

In Hollywood, behind every successful husband is another woman.

Hollywood: Where a pal is someone who is around when he needs you.

Hollywood: Where everyone is a genius until he loses his job.

Hollywood: Where the people accept you for what you're not.

Hollywood: Where society moves in the best triangles.

Hollywood: Where they live happily, and get married ever afterward.

Race tracks attract people who have a talent for picking the wrong horse.

Many things run into money, except the horses I bet on.

The horse is a friend of man—until you start betting on him.

Woman's intuition never works at the race track either.

That's Entertainment

My horse was so late getting home, he tiptoed into the stable.

I know a fellow who always makes money at the track—he's a jockey.

Television helps you meet new people—
especially repairmen.

Giant screen television makes a bad program much worse.

Humor, like history, repeats itself.

I've been in show business thirty years, and I have the jokes to prove it.

His jokes are not funny, but his delivery is terrible.

Women must have a sense of humor—look at the men they marry.

Whenever I tell jokes, I get carried away.

Altered States . . . Of Mind

You have a ready wit. Let me know when it's ready.

I don't believe in reincarnation, but what were you when you were alive?

How can you talk all night without stopping to think?

You appear to be as happy as if you were in your right mind.

I'm paid to make an idiot out of myself. Why do you do it for free?

Are you naturally stupid or are you waiting for a brain transplant?

If it pays to be ignorant, why are you always broke?

Why don't you sit down and rest your brains?

I enjoy talking to you. My mind needs a rest.

Dieting won't help her—no diet will reduce a fat head.

Many doctors have examined his head, but they can't find anything.

The more I think of you the less I think of you.

Show me a bigot, and I'll show you a man who is certain of something he knows nothing about.

Conscience is a mother-in-law whose visit never ends.

The conscience is a thinking man's filter.

He's a great talker—the best you can ever hope to escape from.

Dumb? If anyone said "Hello" to her she would be stuck for an answer.

His final decision seldom tallies with the one immediately following it.

He has a brain, but it hasn't reached his head.

Man is the only animal that speaks, except when he talks like an ass.

She has a pretty little head. For a head, it's pretty little.

He has a one-track mind, and the traffic on it is very light.

If you want a thing to be well done, don't do it yourself.

Altered States . . . Of Mind

He doesn't know his own mind—and he hasn't missed much.

They've named a town after him: Marblehead, Massachusetts.

He isn't scatterbrained. He hasn't any brains to scatter.

The only way she can make up her mind is to powder her forehead.

He has a strange growth on his neck—his head.

He's studying to be a moron.

My girlfriend has no more on her mind than anywhere else.

He's so stupid he can't spell LSD.

This idiot took the screens off her windows to let the flies out.

I finally had to move from Massachusetts. I couldn't spell it.

It takes my wife an hour to cook Minute rice.

If ignorance is bliss, why aren't more people happy?

There's no fool like an old fool, except an older fool.

The only thing my mother-in-law ever read was an eye-chart.

If she said what she thought, she'd be speechless.

It's all right to be dumb, but he's making a career of it.

My brother would have to climb Mt. Everest to reach a deep thought.

He lost his mind when a butterfly kicked him in the head.

When he gets an idea into his head, he has the whole thing in a nutshell.

She thinks blood vessels are some kind of ship.

Imagine a guy who needed a tutor to pass recess.

She spent two days in a revolving door looking for a doorknob.

Success turned his head, and it left him facing in the wrong direction.

Every so often you meet a man whose ignorance is encyclopedic.

When our gas pipe was leaking she put a pan under it.

He walked through a screen door and strained himself.

Too bad they don't sell toupees with brains in them.

He runs around his bed trying to catch some sleep.

He should study to be a bone specialist. He has the head for it.

Daydream: being lost in thought because you are a stranger there.

He manages to keep his head above water—but that's because wood floats.

When a man is wrapped up in himself, he makes a very small package.

If he ever changes his faith, it'll be because he no longer thinks he's God.

An egotist is a self-made man who worships his creator.

A highbrow is a person educated beyond his own intelligence.

Altered States . . . Of Mind

His head is getting too big for his toupee.

He has an alarm clock and a phone—neither rings—they applaud.

He needs a hole in the ground to shrink to his normal proportions.

She had to go to a plastic surgeon to have her nose lowered.

Someone should press the "down" button on his elevator shoes.

He keeps getting carried away by the sound of his own mouth.

He thinks it's a halo, but it's only a swelled head.

He thinks that if he hadn't been born, people would wonder why.

The way she acts, you'd think it was her duty to be snooty.

The hardest opinion she's ever had to keep is her opinion of herself.

Success is going to his head, but it's bound to be a short visit.

Every time he looks in the mirror, he takes a bow.

His bathroom ceiling has a mirror, so he can watch himself gargle.

He's the type who talks big and performs small.

Her head's like a weather vane: easily turned by the slightest wind.

He didn't just grow with responsibility—he bloated.

You could make a fortune renting his head out as a balloon.

Success turned his head. Too bad it didn't wring his neck.

He can pat himself on the back better than a contortionist.

Success has not only gone to his head, but to his mouth, too.

Being egotistical is the only satisfaction some men find in life.

Imagine a girl so dumb, mind readers only charge her half-price.

Altered States . . . Of Mind

A moron is a guy who wrinkles his brow while watching television.

My boss is just as smart as he can be—unfortunately.

I have a neighbor whose mind wanders—unfortunately he just goes along.

After a man reaches 60, his mischief is mainly in his head.

Somehow when two know-it-alls get together, they always disagree.

A smart aleck knows things without having to learn them.

Most men can detect a rattle in the car faster than one in their head.

Many people who think themselves broad-minded, are really thick-headed.

Knowledge is power, but not for the man who knows it all.

Nothing Personal, But . . .

May we have the pleasure of your absence?

I looked high and low for you. I didn't look low enough.

Don't move—I want to forget you just the way you are.

If you have your life to live over again, don't do it.

If you have your life to live over again, do it overseas.

I'd put a curse on you, but somebody beat me to it.

I know this man through thick and thick.

I'd like to say we're glad you're here—I'd like to say it . . .

Someday you'll go too far, and I hope you'll stay there.

Why don't you go to a window and lean out too far?

I know you have to be somebody—but why do you have to be you?

His friends don't know what to give him for Christmas. What do you give
a guy who's had everybody?

He's as spineless as spaghetti.

What got you out of the woodwork?

Why don't you step outside for a few years?

It's good to see you. It means you're not behind my back.

Was the ground cold when you crawled out this morning?

There's only one thing that keeps me from breaking you in half; I don't want two of you around.

If there's ever a price on your head, take it.

Some people bring happiness wherever they go. You bring happiness whenever you go.

Let me tell you about our guest of honor. Never has a man been more sworn at—more spit at—more maligned—and rightfully so!

You're perfect for hot weather. You leave me cold.

Nothing Personal, But . . .

He doesn't have an enemy in the world—he's outlived them all.

I think the world of you—any of you know what condition the world is in today.

I understand you throw yourself into everything you undertake; please go and dig a deep well.

There's a train leaving in an hour. Be under it.

I'll never forget the first time we met—but I'm trying.

If you'll stop telling lies about me I'll stop telling the truth about you.

I don't know what makes you tick, but I hope it's a time bomb.

It's nice hearing from you—next time send me a postcard.

You have a nice personality—but not for a human being.

Look, I'm not going to engage in a battle of wits with you—I never attack anyone who is unarmed.

I'd like to introduce you to some friends of mine. I want to break off with them.

Someday you'll find yourself and will you be disappointed.

I like you—I have no taste, but I like you.

When the grim reaper comes for you he'll have a big smile on his face.

Do me a favor—on your way home, make it a point to jaywalk.

I'd like to run into you again—sometime when you're walking and I'm driving.

If Moses had known you, there would positively have been another commandment.

He lights up a room when he leaves it.

Don't sell him short. In college he was a four letter man and they called him bleep.

Nothing Personal, But . . .

He was a real gentleman. He reminds me of St. Paul—one of the dullest towns in America.

The thing he does for his friends can be counted on his little finger.

The back fence is the shortest distance between two gossips.

Show me a small boy and I'll show you an accessory to the grime.

He never has ups and downs—he always goes around in circles.

He puts up a big bluff and always stumbles over it.

Not even the Missing Persons Bureau could help him find himself.

If I started selling lamps, the sun would stop setting.

He was born with a silver spoon in his mouth, but never made a stir with it.

Any friend of yours is—a friend of yours.

A yawn is nature's way of giving the person listening to a bore an opportunity to open his mouth.

A bore is a person who talks when you want him to listen.

A bore is the kind of guy who always attracts inattention.

A boy becomes a man when he wears out the seat of his pants instead of the soles of his shoes.

Just because a boy is quiet does not mean he is up to mischief; he may be asleep.

If anything is as dirty as a small boy, it's probably his bath towel.

Some people tell all they know, others tell a great deal more.

He should rent his mouth out as a fly catcher.

The chronic complainer is a man whose like is seldom seen.

She has a tongue that could clip a hedge.

Nothing Personal, But . . .

She has a tongue that jaywalks over every conversation.

She talks so much, I get hoarse just listening to her.

Let's have an intelligent conversation. I'll talk and you listen.

He took his time when he spoke. Unfortunately he took ours, too.

He was a soothing speaker. He put me right to sleep.

It's not what she says that hurts—it's the number of times she says it.

He's a regular Rock of Jello.

He's such a lightweight, he could tap-dance on a chocolate eclair.

He always stoops to concur.

His trouble is too much bone in the head and not enough in the back.

He bows and scrapes like a windshield wiper.

He reminds me of a weathercock that turns with every wind.

Henny Youngman's 888 Greatest Insults

Brave? He'll go into the morgue and offer to lick any man in the house.

He gives his conscience a lot of credit that belongs to his cold feet.

When a man pats you on the back, he's figuring where to stick the knife.

A guy who can take it or leave it—mostly takes it.

It's easier to hold an eel by the tail than to pin some men down.

The trouble with some people is that they listen with their mouths.

Any woman who never hears any gossip needs a hearing aid.

Only a teenager talks on the phone long enough to have to change ears.

Tourists all have the same slogan: "Stop, Look, and Litter."

I've been up against the wall so long, the handwriting is on me.

Nothing Personal, But . . .

The only way I'll ever get up in the world is in an airplane.

My boss says I'm giving failure a bad name.

When your ship comes in you'll find your friends on the dock.

At college, he majored in alibiology.

They named the loafer shoe after him.

Imagine! A college boy who is too lazy to write home for money.

Nature provides lazy people with a big cushion to sit around on.

He has an excellent background, and he's always leaning on it.

He's so lazy his feet hurt before he gets out of bed.

He's so lazy he won't even exercise discretion.

Some people look for faults as if they were buried treasure.

I hate those people who tell you off by going on and on.

About the Author

From the London Palladium to Las Vegas clubs, to Miami and Broadway vaudeville houses, over radio and television, and at more Bar Mitzvahs than he cares to recall, millions have rocked with laughter at Henny Youngman's one-liners (and, in a pinch, at his fiddle!). "I started out in this business as a musician," he says, "but I was a lousy fiddler. People used to laugh at me. So I became a comedian."

Born in London and reared in Brooklyn, he entered show business at an early age and discovered that by not turning down any offers, he could work 300 days a year and get rich ("Frank Sinatra once told me that money isn't everything, and I said, 'Quite right, but you can't be rich without it' ").